Introduction To Data Networks:
PDN, LAN, MAN, WAN, and Wireless Data, Technologies and Systems

Lawrence Harte

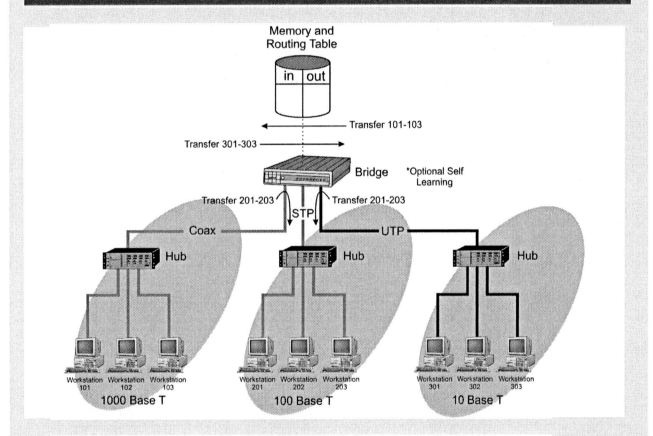

Memory and
Routing Table

in | out

Transfer 101-103

Transfer 301-303

Bridge

*Optional Self
Learning

Transfer 201-203

STP

Transfer 201-203

Coax

UTP

Hub

Hub

Hub

Workstation 101 Workstation 102 Workstation 103

Workstation 201 Workstation 202 Workstation 203

Workstation 301 Workstation 302 Workstation 303

1000 Base T

100 Base T

10 Base T

Excerpted From:

Telecom Systems

ALTHOS Publishing

With Updated Information

About the Author

 Mr. Harte is the president of Althos, an expert information provider covering the communications industry. He has over 29 years of technology analysis, development, implementation, and business management experience. Mr. Harte has worked for leading companies including Ericsson/General Electric, Audiovox/Toshiba and Westinghouse and consulted for hundreds of other companies. Mr. Harte continually researches, analyzes, and tests new communication technologies, applications, and services. He has authored over 30 books on telecommunications technologies on topics including Wireless Mobile, Data Communications, VoIP, Broadband, Prepaid Services, and Communications Billing. Mr. Harte's holds many degrees and certificates include an Executive MBA from Wake Forest University (1995) and a BSET from the University of the State of New York, (1990).

ALTHOS Publishing

ISBN: 0-9742787-3-4

All trademarks are trademarks of their respective owners. We use names to assist in the explanation or description of information to the benefit of the trademark owner and ALTHOS publishing does not have intentions for the infringement of any trademark.

ALTHOS electronic books (ebooks) and images are available for use in educational, promotional materials, training programs, and other uses. For more information about using ALTHOS ebooks and images, please contact Karen Bunn at kbunn@Althos.com or (919) 557-2260

Table of Contents

Data Networks

Data networks are communication systems that are installed and operated exclusively for the transfer of information between data communication devices (such as computers). Data network types include premises distribution networks (PDN's), local area networks (LAN's), metropolitan area networks (MAN's), and wide area networks (WAN's). These are hierarchical with the PAN being the smallest and the WAN being the umbrella architecture.

PANs are short-range data communications systems that are primarily used to interconnect peripheral equipment (such as a mouse or keyboard) with a local computer or computing system. LANs are designed to reliably transfer large amounts of data quickly and error-free over a very small area such as an office. MAN's facilitate LAN-to-LAN information exchange in a local telephone exchange area. The use of a WAN allows for information to be exchanged between LAN's located at significant distances from each other. For example a LAN in Chicago sharing information with a LAN Seattle would do so across a WAN.

A data network is composed of several key parts such as data terminals (e.g., personal computers), network adapters, access wiring, and data distribution nodes (e.g., routers, brouters, and switches.) In some data networks, network management/control systems are used to configure, monitor, coordinate, and control the network elements.

Data Terminals

Data terminals are data input and output devices that are used to communicate with a remotely located computer or other data communication device. Data terminals frequently consist of a keyboard, video display monitor, and communication circuitry that can connect the data terminal with the remotely located computer.

The term "data terminal" is often used to describe multiple types of devices including personal computers (PCs), dedicated "dumb" terminals, scientific workstations, and other types of computers that can communicate with other computers or a host computer.

Data terminal equipment (DTE) is a device that captures and organize (e.g. serialize) information for communication to other communication devices. Data communication equipment (DCE) circuits are assemblies that convert data information into a format that can be transferred through a communication network.

Figure 1 shows how several data terminals (or personal computers operating as data terminals) that are connected through data communication equipment (DCE) to allow a user to receive and send communication through a network to a remote computer. In this diagram, the data terminal allows the user to view information on a monitor and enter information through the keyboard. This data terminal is connected through a combined digital service unit (DSU) and channel service unit (CSU). The DSU/CSU converts the data terminal's digital signals into format that can be sent through a telephone line to a DSU/CSU that communicates with a remote computer.

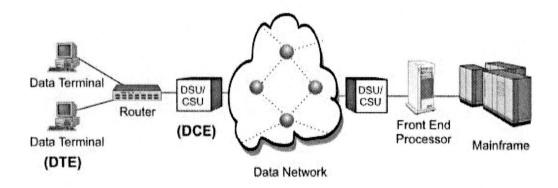

Figure 1, Data Terminals

Network Interface Card (NIC)

A NIC is a device that adapts the data communication network protocol to a data bus or data interface within a computer. The NIC is installed between a computer network (such as the Ethernet) and a computer data bus (such as a PCI socket). The NIC is usually a PC expansion board connector and operating system. Software (NIC drivers) is installed and setup to recognize the NIC card in the computer.

LAN Wiring

There are typically three types of wiring used in LAN systems: twisted pair, coaxial cable (coax), and fiber. Of these, twisted pair is dominant for several reasons: ease of installation, availability, cost, and speed as a function of relative cost.

Twisted pair comes in a variety of "categories" and is either shielded twisted pair (STP) or unshielded twisted pair (UTP). UTP is the less expensive and the most widely used. STP has an outer copper or foil conductor located just beneath the out sheath of the wire. In areas where there is a significant incidence of electromagnetic interference (EMI), such as around factory floor machinery or hospital radiological and medical imaging equipment, STP is used.

Twisted pair wire is classified by categories that relate to the data transmission speed at which the wire is capable of passing data. For each category there are manufacturing specifications such as wire quality, insulation characteristics, and number of twists per inch. Generally, the higher the number of twists, the higher the data transmission rate can be.

Routinely LAN cable is four-pair (eight conductors) even though most data communication systems (such as Ethernet) only require 2 pairs (transmit and receive pairs). It is installed with all conductors terminated on each end into patch fields, hub equipment, or office wall plates (jack fields). From the office wall jack the typical PC or peripheral device is connected to the LAN via a wall cord that is also four-pair terminated in RJ-45 modular connectors. Most offices are wired for multiple network connections and in many cases the voice and data wiring is installed together and to the same cable specification (e.g., category 3 and above).

Network Distribution and Routing

Network distribution and routing equipment provides communication paths between the end-user and the services they desire to use (e.g., Internet). There are three basic methods used to distribute in data networks: broadcast (distribution hubs), dedicated paths (switching nodes), and packet-switching (routers).

Hubs broadcast information to all the communication devices that are connected to it. Switches create a physical or logical connection between data communication devices. Routers are intelligent switches that can dynamically route (switch to other routers) packets of data toward their ultimate destination.

Network Access Control

Network access control is a process of coordinating access of data communication devices to a shared communications media (transmission medium). Network access control is a combination of media access control (MAC) and service authorization.

There are two key ways data communication devices can access communication systems; non-contention based and contention based. Non-contention based regularly poll or schedule data transmission access attempts to communicate thorough the data network. An example of a non-contention based data communication system is token ring. In the token ring system, only the data communication device that has the token is allowed to transmit. This ensures that other data devices will not interfere with the data transmission. Contention based access control systems allow data communication devices to randomly access the system through the sensing and coordination of busy status and detected collisions. Carrier sense multiple access (CSMA) with collision detection (CSMA/CD) or collision avoidance (CSMA/CA) listen to the data activity first to determine if the systems is not busy (carrier sense) before they begin a transmit request. After the device transmits its required, it waits to hear if the system has acknowledged its' request (usually an echo of its original signal.) If the CSMA/CD device does not hear an acknowledgement, it will wait a random amount of time before transmitting another data transmission service request.

The CSMA/CA system differs from the CSMA/CD system by the assignment of different access wait periods to different priority groups of devices. This allows high priority devices (such as a system management data terminal) to attempt access before a lower priority device (e.g., web browsing terminal.)

Figure 2 shows the key ways networks can control data transmission access: non-contention based and contention based. This diagram shows that non-contention based regularly poll or schedule data transmission access attempts before computers can begin to transmit data. This diagram shows that a token is passed between each computer in the network and computers can only transmit when they have the token. Because there is no potential for collisions, computers do not need to confirm the data was successfully transmitted through the network. This diagram also shows contention based access control systems allow data communication devices to randomly access the system through the sensing and coordination of busy status and detected collisions. These devices first listen to see if the system is not busy and then randomly transmit their data. Computers in the contention-based systems must confirm that data was successfully transmitted through the network, because there is the potential for collisions.

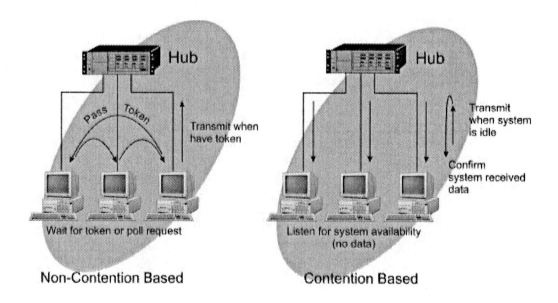

Figure 2, Data Network Access Control

Protocols

Protocols are a precise set of rules, timing, and a syntax that govern the accurate transfer of information between devices or software applications. Key protocols in data transmission networks include access protocols, handshaking, line discipline, and session protocols.

Access protocols are the set of rules that workstations use to avoid collisions when sending information over shared network media. Access protocols are also known as the media access control (MAC) protocols. Handshaking protocols involve the sequence of events that occur between communication devices that negotiate the data transmission rules and ensure reliable data transmission. When data devices begin to communicate, they discover the capabilities and agree on a common set of protocols to use during data communications session. Line discipline is the sequence of events that must occur to control the reception of data, perform error detection and correction, and multiplexing of control information, if necessary. Session protocols control the end-to-end connectivity of a data communication session. Session protocols ensure all the data is received and in the correct order.

Different protocols may be used in systems that provide similar functions. An example of this is token ring and Ethernet. Although these networks may actually use the same signaling system, they use incompatible protocols. To allow data to transfer between these networks, protocol converters are used. Protocol converts receive data and control messages, reformat data and convert control messages, and retransmit the data using the new protocol rules.

Network Management

Network management is set of procedures, equipment, and operations that keep a telecommunications network operating near maximum efficiency despite unusual loads or equipment failures. Network managers should be able to monitor, configure, and operate their network equipment from distant communication locations using a set of network management protocols.

A key network management protocol is simple network management protocol (SNMP). SNMP is an industry standard communication protocol that is used to manage multiple types of network equipment (most vendors comply at some level.) By conforming to SNMP protocol, equipment assemblies that are produced by different manufacturers can be managed by a single network management program. While many vendors supply proprietary configuration and administration software for their products, many support diagnostic and maintenance features through the use of SNMP.

Overview

Data networks can be characterized as premises distribution networks (PDNs), local area networks (LANs), metropolitan area networks (MANs), wide area networks (WANs), and wireless data networks (WDNs).

Premises Distribution Networks (PDN)

A premises distribution network (PDN) is a short-range network that is located at a customer's facility or even within their personal area. A PDN is used to connect terminal equipment (mice and keyboards) to computing and data network equipment. The most common types of PANs are universal serial bus (USB) and FireWire (IEEE-1394). When PDN networks use wireless technology they are called wireless personal area networks (WPAN). Popular types of WPAN systems include Bluetooth and RFHome/SWAP.

PANs are short-range communication networks that have a range of tens or hundreds of feet. They are usually designed to allow one of the connections to operate as a controller (a host) and the other connection(s) to follow the commands of the host (a slave). PANs typically have data transfer rates from 1 Mbps (wireless) to 480 Mbps (wired).

Figure 3 shows several popular forms of PDNs. This diagram shows that the data transfer rate varies with the length and type of interconnection cable. This diagram also shows that some PDN systems have multiple versions and that these versions have different data transfer rates.

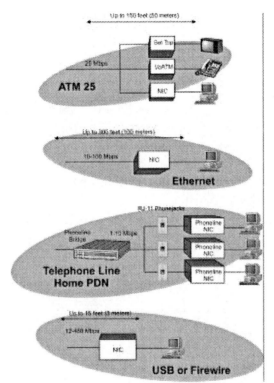

Figure 3, Premises Distribution Network (PDN) Types

Local Area Networks (LANs)

Local area networks (LANs) are private data communication networks that used high-speed digital communications channels for the interconnection of computers and related equipment in a limited geographic area. LANs can use fiber optic, coaxial, twisted-pair cables, or radio transceivers to transmit and receive data signals. LAN's are networks of computers, normally personal computers, connected together in close proximity (office setting) to each other in order to share information and resources. The two predominant LAN architectures are token ring and Ethernet. Other LAN technologies are ArcNet, AppleTalk, and fiber distributed data interface (FDDI). When local area networks use wireless technology, they are called wireless local area networks (WLANs). Popular WLANs include 802.11 and HyperLAN.

LANs are medium-range communication networks that have a range of hundreds to thousands of feet. They are usually designed to allow each device to operate independently (peer to peer). LANs typically have data transfer rates from 2 Mbps (wireless) to 10 Gbps (optical).

Figure 4 shows several of the most popular LAN topologies and their configurations. Some data networks are setup as bus networks (all computers share the same bus), as start networks (computers connect to a central data distribution node), or as a ring (data circles around the ring). This diagram shows for popular types of LAN networks: Ethernet, token ring, FDDI, and wireless LAN (WLAN) networks.

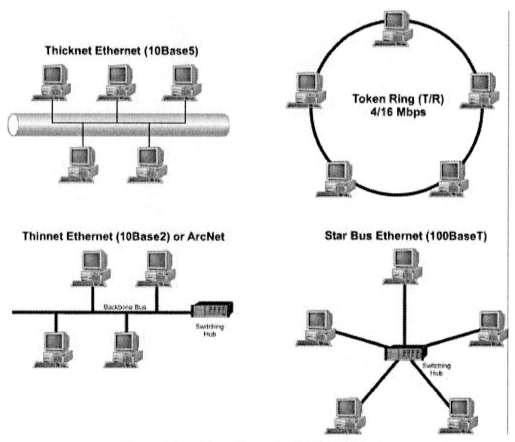

Figure 4, Local Area Networks (LANs) Topologies

Metropolitan Area Networks (MAN's)

A MAN is a data communications network or interconnected groups of data networks that have geographic boundaries of a metropolitan area. MANs are used to connect networks that are totally or partially segregated from other networks. MAN's offer the ability to connect networks across a metropolitan area as if they were co-located in the same building or on the same campus. To create a MAN, businesses install or lease communications links between the LANs. The backbone interconnection for a MAN is routinely high capacity fiber-based systems. This provides a fairly high data transfer rate and provides a high degree of fault tolerance. MAN's commonly use dual ring fiber systems that are self-healing (automatic connection re-routing) to allow uninterrupted communication if fiber line is cut or damaged.

Figure 5 shows a five node MAN connecting that connects several LAN systems via a FDDI system. This diagram shows that each LAN may be connected within the MAN using different technology such as T1/E1 copper access lines, digital subscriber line (DSL), coax, microwave, or fiber connections. In each case, a router provides a connection from each LAN to connect to the MAN.

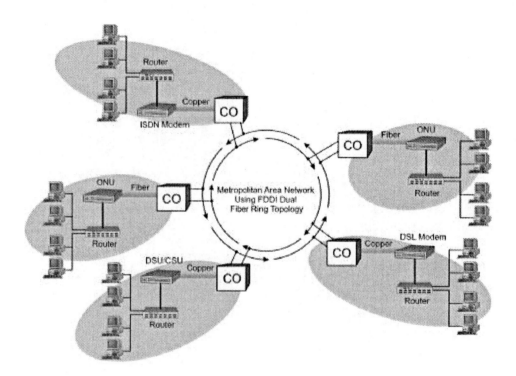

Figure 5, Metropolitan Area Networks (MANs)

Wide Area Networks (WAN's)

WANs are communication networks that provide data transmission services through large geographically separate areas. A WAN can be established by linking together two or more metropolitan area networks, which enables data terminals in one city to access data resources in another city or country. When wide area networks use wireless technologies, they are commonly called mobile data networks (MDNs).

Figure 6 shows that a WAN is usually composed of several different data networks such as PDNs, LANs, and MANs. Different types of communication lines such as leased lines (dedicated connections), packet data systems, or fiber transmission lines can interconnect these networks. WANs may be interconnected to and/or through the public switched telephone network (PSTN) or public packet data networks (such as the Internet).

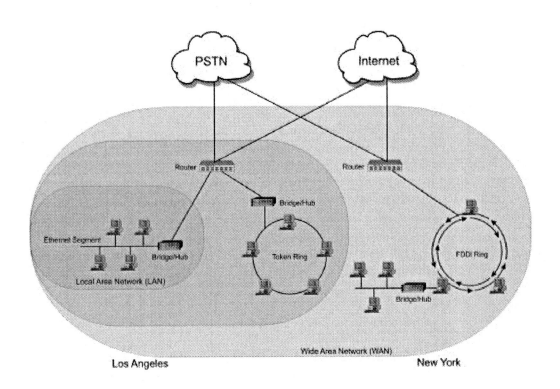

Figure 6, Wide Area Networks (WAN's)

Wireless Data Networks

Wireless data networks allow computers and other types of data processing devices to communicate with each other using radio propagation as the transmission medium. There are three key types of wireless data networks; wireless personal area networks (WPANs), wireless local area networks (WLANs), and mobile data networks (MDNs).

Wireless personal area networks (WPANs) are temporary (ad-hoc) short-range wireless communication systems that typically connect personal accessories such as headsets, keyboards, and portable devices to communications equipment and networks.

Wireless LANs can be an extension of an existing wired LAN or it can be the only interconnection used by the data new network. While adaptable to both indoor and outdoor environments, wireless LANs are especially suited for indoor locations such as office buildings, manufacturing floors, hospitals and universities. Wireless LAN's generally use either infrared or radio frequency (RF) as their transmission media. Infrared is line-of-sight only, and poses problems in many office environments when viewed as a single solution. RF is not line-of-sight and thus is not subject to the problems of infrared. However, wireless LANs may encounter interference from other devices found in the office or factory that can reduce the data transmission speed for all devices within the network. WLAN systems typically transmit data up to 54 Mbps (2-11 Mbps is more typical).

Wide area wireless systems (also called Mobile Data Networks) such as cellular, PCS, or public packet radio systems, provide wireless data service to relatively large geographic areas. Until the late 1990s, wide area mobile data transmission rates have been usually limited to below 28 kbps due to their relatively high usage cost of 10 cents per kilobyte ($100 per megabyte). Due to the evolution of modulation technologies and data transmission protocols, wide area wireless data transmission rates have increased to over 100 kbps with a cost of approximately $1 to $3 per megabyte.

Point-to-point wireless data systems may be used to interconnect data networks between buildings within a campus. Providing this wireless data link only requires the installation of 2 antennas with a clear line of site communication. Point-to-point microwave data transmission rates can exceed 45 Mbps.

Figure 7 shows the three key types of wireless data networks; WPAN, WLAN, and wide area Mobile Data. The laptop computers in the first building use a low power (1 mWatt) wireless PAN (WPAN) to transfer audio to wireless headsets. This diagram shows a wireless LAN system that has multiple access nodes. These access nodes operate as gateways between the data communication devices (e.g., mobile computer) and the data network hub. Building 1 uses an older 802.11 wireless LAN system that operates from 902-928 MHz at 2 Mbps. Building 2 uses a newer 802.11 wireless LAN system that operates at 2.4 GHz providing up to 11 Mbps data transfer rate. A microwave data link provides a 45 Mbps interconnection between building 1 and building 2. Finally, a user who is operating in a remote area outside the core campus is using the wide area mobile system to transfer data files (at a data transfer rate below 28 kbps).

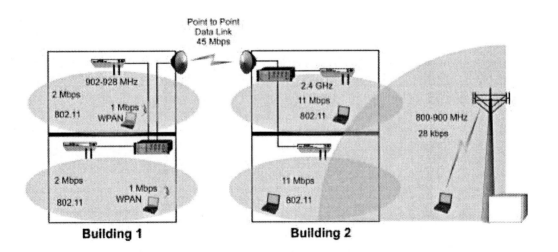

Figure 7, Wireless Data Networks

Technologies

The key technologies that have emerged to enable data networks include data modems, hubs, bridges, routers, gateways, and firewalls.

Data Modems

Data modems are devices that convert signals between analog and digital formats for transfer to other types of communication lines. Data modems are used to transfer data signals over conventional analog telephone lines. The term modem also may refer to a device or circuit that converts analog signals from one frequency band to another.

A single connection (point-to-point) analog data circuit requires a modem at each end to transfer digital signals. The type of modems used on each end must be compatible due to encoding and decoding processes. Analog communication lines are restricted to audio bandwidth of 300 Hz to 3300 HZ. To communicate digital data and control signals, the modems vary the frequency of the carrier in each direction based on an agreed to algorithm for encoding bits.

Figure 8 shows a modem with its functional responsibilities listed. From the DTE (serial interface RS 232-C) to the line the modem performs a digital-to-analog conversion and from the line to the DTE an analog-to-digital conversion.

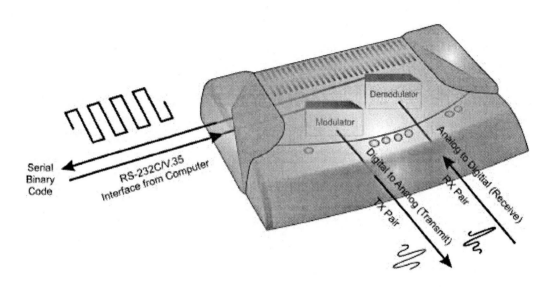

Figure 8, Data Modem

Digital Service Unit (DSU)/Channel Service Unit (CSU)

DSU/CSU's are the digital equivalent of the analog modem and are translation codecs (COde and DECode) coupled with a network termination interface (NTI). DSU/CSU's operate only in a digital environment. DSUs/CSUs work together to reformat and channelize digital signals for transmission on multiple channel lines.

Hub

A hub is a communication device that distributes communication to several devices in a network through the re-broadcasting of data that it has received from one (or more) of the devices connected to it. A hub generally is a simple device that re-distributes data messages to multiple receivers. However, hubs can include switching functional and multi-point routing connection and other advanced system control functions. Hubs can be passive or active. Passive hubs simply re-direct (re-broadcast) data it receives. Active hubs both receive and regenerate the data it receives.

Figure 9 shows an Ethernet hub. This diagram shows that one of the computers has sent a data message to the hub on its transmit lines. The hub receives the data from the device and rebroadcasts the information on all of

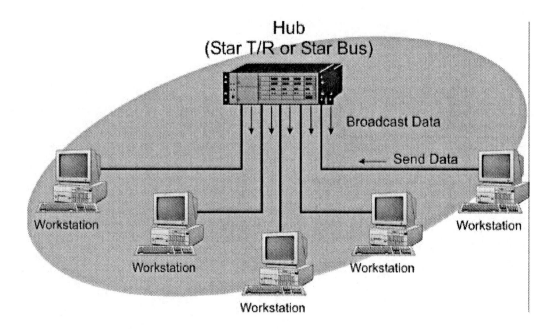

Figure 9, Ethernet Hub Operation

its transmit lines, including the line that the data was received on. The hub's receiver and transmit lines are reversed from the computers. This allows computers that are connected to the hub to hear the information on through receive lines. The sending computer uses the echo of its own information as confirmation the hub has successfully received and retransmitted its information. This indicates that no collision has occurred with other computers that may have transmitted information at the same time.

Bridge

A bridge is a data communication device that connects two or more segments of data communication networks by forwarding packets between them. The bridge operates as a physical connector and buffer between similar types of networks.

Bridges extend the reach of the LAN from one segment to another. Bridges have memory that allows them to store and forward packets. Bridges are protocol independent as the do not perform protocol adaptations.

Bridges contain a packet address-forwarding table (routing table) that they use to determine if the packets should be forwarded between networks. A network administrator may initially program the packet-forwarding table or it can be programmed through the discovery of packet addresses (self-learned) that are received by the bridge. A self-learning bridge monitors the packet traffic in the network to continually update its packet-forwarding table.

Bridges primarily operate at the physical layer and link layers of the OSI reference model. A bridge receives packets from one network, review the address of the packet to determine if it should be routed to the other network(s) it is connected to, and retransmits the packet following the standard protocol rules for the systems it is connected to.

Figure 10 shows the basic operation of a bridge that is connecting 3 segments of a LAN network. Segment 1 of the LAN has addresses 101 through 103, segment 2 of the LAN has addresses 201 through 203, and segment 3 of the LAN has addresses 301 through 303. The table contained in the bridge indicates the address ranges that should be forwarded to specific ports. This diagram shows a packet that is received from LAN segment 3 that contains the address 102 will be forwarded to LAN segment 1. When a data packet from computer 303 contains the address 301, the bridge will receive the packet but the bridge will ignore (not forward) the packet.

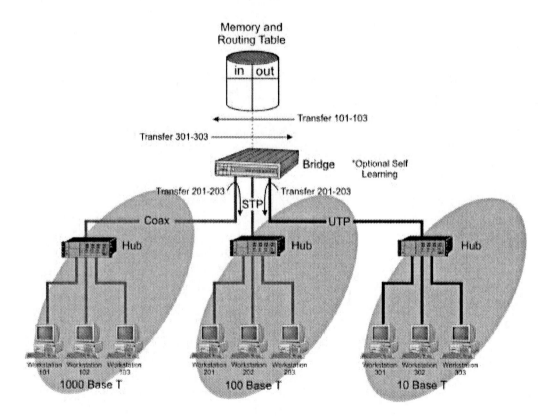

Figure 10, Data Bridge Operation

Routers

A router is a device that directs (routes) data from one path to another in a network. Routers base their switching information on one or more information parameters contained within the packet of data they receive. These parameters may include the destination address, availability of a transmission path or communications channel, maximum allowable amount of transmission delay a packet can accept, along with other key parameters. Routers that connect data paths between different types of networks are sometimes called gateways.

Routers provide some of the same functionality as network switches. Their primary function is to provide a path for each routable packet to its destination. When a router is initially installed into a network, it begins its life by requesting a data network address. Using this data network address, it sends (broadcasts) messages to nearby routers and begins to store address connections of routers that are located around it. Routers regularly exchange their connection information (lists of devices it is connected to) with nearby routers to help them keep the latest packet routing information.

A router can make decisions on where to forward packets dependent on a variety of factors including the maximum transmission distance or packet priority. Distance vector routing and link state routing allow the router to select paths that match the needs of the data that is being sent through it.

Some routers may use fixed (static) routing tables that are manually programmed by the network administrator instead of dynamically created routing tables. The use of static routing tables may seem to be inflexible, however the use of static routing ensures other router's that may have corrupt routing tables are not able to change or influence the routing table.

Figure 11 shows a how a router can dynamically forward packets toward their destination. This diagram shows that a router contains a routing table (database) that dynamically changes. This diagram shows a router with address 100 is connected to two other routers with addresses 800 and 900. Each of these routers periodically exchanges information allowing them to build routing tables that allow them to forward packets they receive. This diagram shows that when router 100 receives a packet for a device number 952, it will forward the packet to router 900. Router 900 will then receive that packet and forward it on to another router that will help that packet reach its destination.

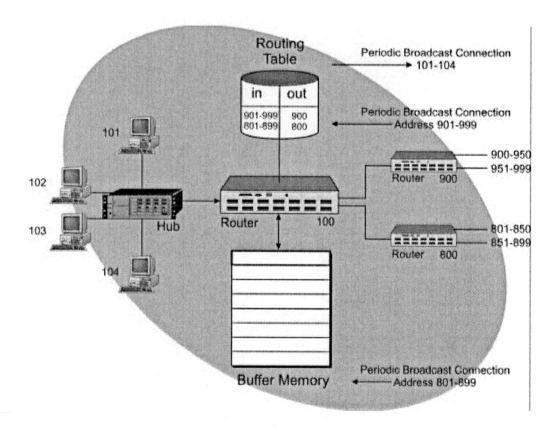

Figure 11, Data Router

Gateways

Gateways are devices that process information (data) or services that is exchanged between two dissimilar computer systems or data networks. A gateway reformats data and protocols in such a way that the two systems or networks can communicate. Gateways can convert packets between dissimilar networks. Because networks may have different types of addressing or offer different types of services, gateways can convert one form of service (such as standard telephone signals) into another form of service (such as IP telephone signals).

Figure 12 shows how a gateway can convert large packets from a FDDI into very small packets in an ATM network. Not only does the gateway have to divide the packets, it must also convert the addresses and control messages into formats that can be understood on both networks.

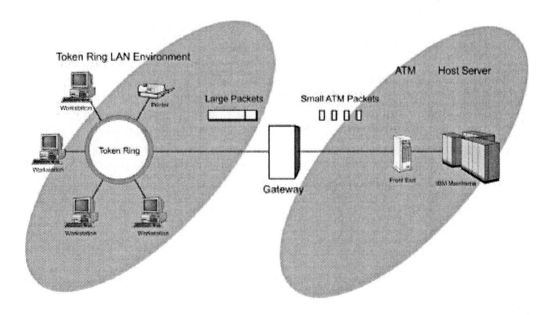

Figure 12, Data Gateway Operation

Firewall

A firewall is a device or software program that runs on a computer that provides protection from external network intruders by inhibiting the transfer of unauthorized packets and by allowing through packets that meet safe criteria. There are various processes that can be used by firewalls to determine which packets are authorized and packets that should be rejected (not forwarded).

Because firewalls can use many different types of analysis to determine packets that will be rejected, they can be complicated to setup. If a firewall is not setup correctly, it can cause problems for users that are sending and expected return packets that may be blocked by the firewall. Because firewalls process and analyze information, this process requires additional time and this can slow down network data transfer and response time.

Figure 13 shows how a firewall works. This diagram shows that a user with address 201 is communicating through a firewall with address 301 to an external computer that is connected to the Internet with address 401. When user 201 sends a packet to the Internet requesting a communications session with computer 401, the packet first passes through the firewall and the firewall notes that computer 201 has requested a communication session, what the port number is, and sequence number of the packet. When packets are received back from computer 401, they are actually addressed to the firewall 301. Firewall 301 analyzes the address and other information in the data packet and determines that it is an expected response to the session computer 201 has initiated. Other packets that are received by the firewall that do not contain the correct session and sequence number will be rejected.

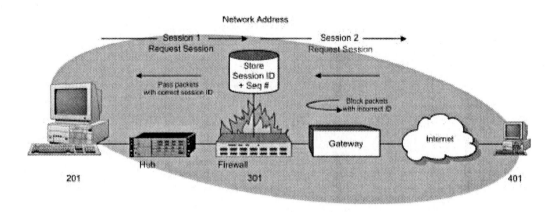

Figure 13, Firewall Operation

The types of firewalls can vary from simple software programs to sophisticated hardware devices. Low-cost software packages and automatic firewall hardware equipment offer a moderate level of increased security. They cannot stop all hackers, but they will stop some of them.

Data Communications Systems

There are many types of wired and wired public and private data communication systems. Some of the more popular data communication systems used include Ethernet, token ring, fiber distributed data interface (FDDI), asynchronous transfer mode 25 (ATM 25), phone line networking (HomePNA), universal serial bus (USB), and Firewire. Some of the popular wireless data communication systems include 802.11 and general packet radio service (GPRS). These data networks are commonly interconnected through the Internet.

Ethernet

Ethernet is a packet-switching transmission protocol that is used in LANs and short to medium range data communication systems. Ethernet is often characterized by its data transmission rate and type of transmission medium (e.g., twisted pair is T and fiber is F). Ethernet systems in 1972 operated at 1 Mbps. In 1992, Ethernet progressed to 10 Mbps data transfer speed (called 10 Base T). In 2001, Ethernet data transfer rates included 100 Mbps (100 BaseT) and 1 Gbps (1000 Base T). In the year 2000, 10 Gigabit fiber Ethernet prototypes had been demonstrated.

Ethernet can be provided on twisted pair, coaxial cable, wireless, or fiber cable. In 2003, the common wired connections for Ethernet was 10 Mbps, 100 Mbps, and 1000 Mbps (1 Gbps). 100 Mbps Ethernet (100 BaseT) is commonly called "Fast Ethernet" and 1000 BaseT is commonly called "Gigabit Ethernet." Wireless Ethernet systems have data transmission rates that are usually limited from 2 Mbps to 54 Mbps.

Ethernet is the older than token ring and is based on linear bus technology. Originally installed using RG-6/8 coaxial cable (called "thicknet"), it was used for high-speed bus applications to interconnect mainframes and mini-computers. With the growth of personal computer (PC) workstations in the 80's and early 90's, a new wiring strategy was implemented using thinner RG-58 coaxial cable (called "thinnet"). In the mid-90's newer twisted pair standards were set and higher speeds were achieved. 10 Mbps (10BaseT) became achievable on Category 3 unshielded twisted pair (UTP) wire.

Because Ethernet systems can use different cabling systems (e.g., fiber, coaxial cable, and twisted pair wire), network interface cards (NICs) must contain a connector that is compatible with the cabling systems. To allow connection to different types of cabling systems, some NIC cards come with multiple connectors. The different types of connectors include a DB-15 AUI connector for thicknet (large coax), BNC coaxial connector for thinnet (thin coax), and RJ-45 (telephone type modular plug) for twisted pair.

Figure 14 shows the operational function of an Ethernet system. Ethernet uses carrier sensing multiple access with collision detection (CSMA/CD) to coordinate access to the network. CSMA/CD is a carrier sense multiple access transmission scheme in which transmission collisions are followed the transmitting stations backing off the network a random amount of time before attempting to retransmit. CSMA/CD is used as the basis of Ethernet networks.

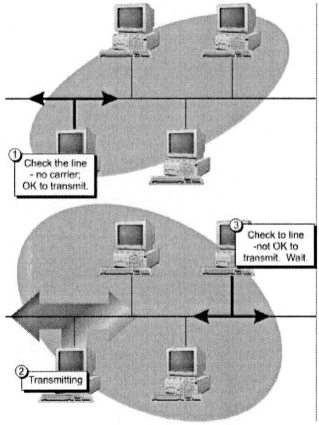

Figure 14, Ethernet System Operation

Token Ring

Token ring is a LAN system developed by IBM that passes a token to each computer connected to the network. Holding of the token permits the computer to transmit data. The token ring specification is IEEE 802.5 and token ring data transmission speed range from 4 Mbps or 16 Mbps. 100 Mbps and higher token ring speeds are in development.

Token ring networks are non-contention based systems, as each computer connected via the token ring network must have received and hold a token before it can transmit. This ensures computers will not transmit data at the same time. Token ring systems provide an efficient control system when many computers are interconnected with each other. This is the reason token ring systems will not see data traffic degradation when many new users are added compared to Ethernet systems. However, passing tokens does add overhead (additional control messages) that reduces the overall data transmission bandwidth of the system.

The token ring LAN architecture was invented by IBM and touted to be the standard for clients of IBM mainframes who sought to replace aging 3270 terminals with LAN's. IBM also developed cabling standards along with hub-like devices called multi-station access units (MAU's). The original MAU's formed a star network with the client PC's and simulated the ring internally. The PC's were connected to the MAU via IBM category type 1, 2, or 3 cable.

Figure 15 shows a typical token ring LAN. This diagram shows that the network is logically setup in a ring and each computer in the token ring network must receive a token before it can transmit. Since the token is relatively small compared to the packets of data that are sent, the token can rapidly move from computer to computer. When a computer receives a token, it can transmit data for a limited amount of time before it is required to forward the token.

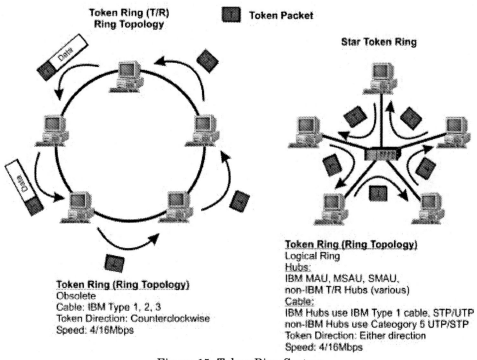

General:
Specified by IEE 802.5
Protocol: Singular token passing
Standard Speeds: 4Mbps, 16Mbps, and 100Mbps

Token Ring (T/R)
Ring Topology

Token Packet

Star Token Ring

Token Ring (Ring Topology)
Logical Ring
Hubs:
IBM MAU, MSAU, SMAU,
non-IBM T/R Hubs (various)
Cable:
IBM Hubs use IBM Type 1 cable, STP/UTP
non-IBM Hubs use Cateogory 5 UTP/STP
Token Direction: Either direction
Speed: 4/16Mbps

Token Ring (Ring Topology)
Obsolete
Cable: IBM Type 1, 2, 3
Token Direction: Counterclockwise
Speed: 4/16Mbps

Figure 15, Token Ring System

Fiber Distributed Data Interface (FDDI)

Fiber distributed data interface (FDDI) is a computer network protocol that uses fiber optic cable as the transmission medium to provide high-speed data transmission service to LANs. FDDI is a token protocol. The basic transmission rate of FDDI is 100 Mbps. FDDI is commonly used as a backbone network that interconnects several LANs within a company. The FDDI specification is IEEE 802.2 and FDDI data transmission speed range from 100 to 200 Mbps. 1000 Mbps and higher FDDI speeds are in development.

FDDI is a LAN architecture that is based on redundant fiber rings that transmit in opposite directions. One of the rings is the primary ring and the other ring is the secondary ring. When the primary ring ceases to be operational (such as a cut cable) the network reconfigures itself (called "self-healing") and it reconfigures the secondary ring as the primary ring.

Both single mode fiber and multimode fiber cable systems can be used with FDDI. Multimode fibers have a wider optical bandwidth transmission capability. However, this introduces distortion and limits the maximum distance for multimode fiber systems to about 2 kilometers. Single mode fiber systems have maximum range of approximately 60 km.

FDDI is a token passing architecture differing from token ring in that while a station has a token it can transmit as many frames as possible before the token expires. Because of this, there can be multiple frames on the ring at any time.

The interconnection devices in a FDDI network include a dual attached concentrator (DAC) and dual attached station (DAS). These devices remove and insert data to the FDDI ring. Each of these devices has dual transmission capability. If the fiber ring is cut, they can automatically redirect data onto its other channel (the secondary ring).

The DAC is a concentrator the converts the optical data on the FDDI system into another format that can be used to connect to other data networks. This allows one FDDI network node to connect to many other data communication devices.

Figure 16 shows FDDI system that uses dual rings that transmit data in opposite directions. This diagram shows one dual attached station (DAS) and a dual attached concentrator (DAC). The DAS receives and forwards the token to the mainframe computer. The DAC receives and token and coordinates its distribution to multiple data devices that are connected to it.

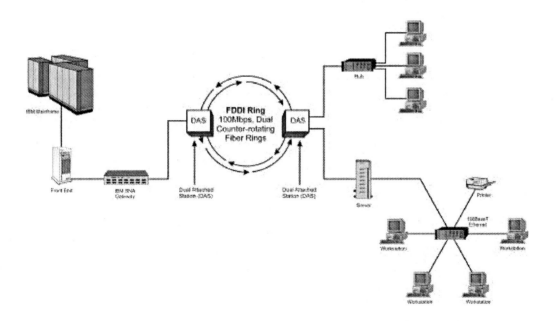

Figure 16, Fiber Distributed Data Interface (FDDI) System

Internet

The Internet is a public data network that interconnects private and government computers. The Internet transfers data from point-to-point by packets that use Internet protocol (IP). Each transmitted packet in the Internet finds its way through the network switching through nodes (computers). Each node in the Internet forwards received packets to another location (another node) that is closer to its destination. Each node contains routing tables that provide packet-forwarding information. The Internet was designed to allow continuous data communication in the event some parts of the network were disabled. The World Wide Web (WWW) is an application on the Internet that allows users to graphically navigate through computers that are connected to the Internet.

The Internet is a network of networks. Although these networks communicate with each other using many different languages (protocols), they all agree to transport data within their network according to a common Internet communication language called transmission control protocol/Internet protocol (TCP/IP). TCP/IP is a set of protocols developed by the U.S. Department of Defense (US DOC) that facilitate the interconnection of dissimilar computer systems across networks. The TCP protocol coordinates the overall flow of data during a data communication session between points (nodes) in the Internet.

IP is an addressing structure that allows packets of data to be routed (redirected) as they migrate through different networks to reach their ultimate destination. Each network receives packets of data in a format that is compatible with the Internet (IP address followed by control and data information) and they encapsulate (place the whole Internet data message into their own data packet format (including the IP address and control information). This allows IP data packets (called "datagrams") to be sent through the network regardless of their actual length or format.

Figure 17 shows that the Internet is the network of networks and it communicates using the universal protocol language TCP/IP. This diagram shows a user who is sending email through the Internet. In this diagram, the application is email. The data from the email is divided into packets and given sequence number by TCP protocol. The destination address is appended to each packet by the IP layer. The IP packets are then sent through an Ethernet LAN by encapsulating the IP datagram within the Ethernet data packet. When the data packet is extracted from the Ethernet, it is placed on the E1 transmission line. When the IP data packet reaches the ATM network, it is subdivided into very small 53 byte data packets that travel through the ATM network. When the ATM packets reach their destination in the ATM network, the original IP datagram is recreated and transferred via the T1 communication line. The T1 communication line interfaces to another Ethernet data network. This Ethernet data network encapsulates the IP datagram and forwards it on to the NIC of the receiving computer. The NIC of the receiving computer removes the IP address and reassembles the IP data packets to form the original email message.

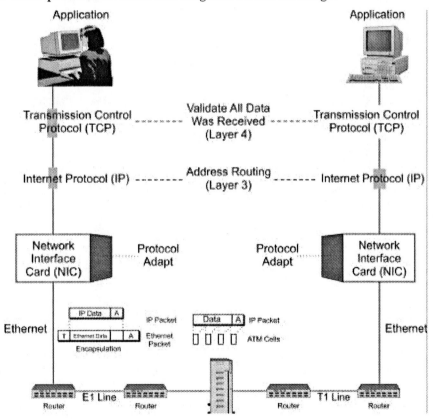

Figure 17, Internet Data Routing

Asynchronous Transfer Mode 25 (ATM 25)

ATM 25 is a low-speed (25 Mbps) version of the asynchronous transfer mode (ATM) system. ATM technology is relatively complex when compared to Ethernet and token ring systems. As a result, the use of standard ATM technology in LAN systems has been limited. However, a 25 Mbps version of the ATM standard was developed for PDN LANs. The capability of ATM systems to simultaneously provide multiple communication channels with varying levels of quality of service (QoS) make it advantageous for use in multimedia systems. ATM 25 technology is used to provide digital video and Internet access through the use of ATM in digital subscriber line (DSL) and cable modem systems.

Phoneline Networking

In the late 1990's, the home phoneline network alliance (HomePNA) developed a specification that allows home computers and data devices (such as network printers) to interconnect via standard home telephone wiring. In the first generation of phoneline networking, data rates of 1 Mbps were achieved but recently data transmission rates of 10 Mbps have been demonstrated. The Phoneline Network uses special NIC's that send and receive high frequency signals that do not interfere with standard telephone service. To connect a phoneline network to a DSL connection, a phoneline bridge must be used.

Universal Serial Bus (USB)

Universal serial bus (USB) is a short distance data communication interface (typically, only a few meters) that now comes standard on most personal computers. The USB was designed to replace the older slower UART data communications port. USB ports permit data transmission speeds up to 12 Mbps. Most computers that were manufactured in 2001 included a universal serial bus (USB) connector. The USB data bus can also connect up to 10 devices to the same bus using a low cost hub device. USB lines can only extend for a few feet from the computer.

FireWire

FireWire is a short distance data communications interface (up to approximately 5 meters) that is based on industry standard IEEE-1394. FireWire can transmit at speeds up to 400 Mbps and can support up to 63 devices per bus. Firewire provides for isochronous (repetitive streaming data format) that allows it to transfer audio and video signals.

Services

Some of the key services provided by data network operators include Internet service provider (ISP) and virtual private networks (VPNs).

Internet Service Provider (ISP)

Internet service provider is a company that provides an end user with data communication service that allows them to connect to the Internet. An ISP purchases a high-speed link to the Internet and divides up the data transmission to allow many more users to connect to the Internet. Internet service providers provide a gateway between end-users and the Internet. For this service, an ISP usually charges a monthly access fee and may charge for the amount of time or amount of data transferred during the billing period.

Virtual Private Networks (VPN's)

Virtual private networks (VPN) network operators provide data connections to companies to allow interconnection of data networks. Companies use VPN to create MANs or WANs.

The best examples of VPN's today are ATM and frame relay networks that connect multiple client sites on what appears to be dedicated circuits. In these networks, data is routed through the VPN network using routing algorithms that transfer data based on congestion and priorities. Because of the speed and fault-tolerance of the VPN provider network, the client company operates as if the inter-site connections were dedicated circuits.

Future Enhancements

Future enhancements for data communication networks include increased data transmission speed, LAN telephony, and storage area networks (SANs).

10 Gigabit Ethernet (10 GE)

10 Gigabit Ethernet (10 GE) is a data communication system that combines Ethernet technology with fiberoptic cable transmission to provide data communication transmission at 10 Gbps (10,000 Mbps). The specifications for 10 GE are being developed by the Gigabit Ethernet Alliance. The Gigabit Ethernet Alliance is a group of companies that was formed in January 2000.

LAN Telephony

LAN telephony (sometimes called TeLANophy) use LAN systems to transport voice communications. LAN telephone technology is a merging of packetized voice with the high-speed data transmission ability of LAN systems. The ability to share data networks with voice systems offers significant cost reduction for telephone services.

LAN telephone system consists of LAN telephones, a data network, a LAN call processing system, and a voice gateway to the PSTN. LAN telephones convert audio into digitized packets that are transferred on the LAN to the call processing computer (CTI system). Each LAN telephone has its own network data address that is related to its telephone number or extension number.

LAN telephones can be integrated into computers or they can be standard along telephones that use LAN protocols that communicate with the systems. In 2001, there were several manufacturers producing IP telephones.

Storage Area Networks (SANs)

Storage area networks (SANs) distribute data and other information to multiple storage devices that are interconnected by data networks. SANs allow for the sharing of resources and pooling of information in the form of shared files at both the server level and the client (individual PC) level. Storage area networks (SAN's) provide fault-tolerant operation through the use redundant data storage in multiple locations. If a failure occurs in one data storage device, other redundant data storage devices may automatically be used as the backup source of information.

Research
Getting Hard to Find Information

Many firms provide general industry specific numbers and information. Althos provides more specific, customized "real-time" intelligence. Typically this includes information that is not generally available to the public.

TOP SECRET

Althos Research performs **Custom Research** and **Industry Specific** Research primarily for the voice and data communication industries. Custom Research is performed to **Answer Specific Questions** or information needs of an individual company. Custom information is typically very specific and often involves the finding and analysis of sensitive information or **Hard to Acquire Data**. Industry Specific Research is typically in the form of more generic research reports.

Market Information	Competitive Analysis	Product Information
Market Share Industry Trends Distribution Channels Emerging Markets Qualified Sales Lead Lists	Production Costs Marketing Costs Future Product Plans Production Capability Organizational Structures	Ability to Manufacture Technology Licensing Supplier Listings Product Matrix Feature Benefit Analysis

Get Answers to Your Specific Questions
Find Information that is not Readily Available
Gather Data to Assist in Business Decisions
Find New Business Opportunities

Althos Research, 404 Wake Chapel Road, Fuquay NC 27526 USA
1-919-557-2260 1-800-227-9681 Fax 1-919-557-2261 WWW.Althos.com
Email: Info@Althos.com

Typical Costs

Custom Research

ALTHOS typically estimates custom research projects as a fixed cost to the customer. This minimizes the risk to the customer that the information may not be readily available and ALTHOS will have to work harder (longer) to obtain the information. ALTHOS usually estimates the cost using our average consulting rate based on the forecasted time to acquire and package the information.

Consulting and Expert Witness

ALTHOS offers various levels of consulting; market, technical and strategic. The cost for consulting varies with the skill level of the consultant. The average research consulting fee ALTHOS charges is $110 per hour. Consulting fees for specific experts can range from $85 per hour for industry analysts to $300 for strategic or technical experts.

Most research projects do not require travel expenses. However, if travel expenses must be incurred by ALTHOS in conjunction with the project (typically for an on-site training session or presentation), travel expenses will be reimbursed on the basis of actual cost. All travel expenses will be approved by the client prior to commitment.

Industry Reports

ALTHOS desires to provide the information to the customer at the lowest cost possible to ensure a satisfied client. If information is available in a industry report, ALTHOS will recommend the purchase or summary analysis of the report whenever it may provide a lower cost.

How Does ALTHOS Do It?

Gathering sensitive information legitimately is an art. It involves dealing with many information sources including former employees and competitors. Most companies want to isolate themselves from this information search process for practical and legal reasons.

ALTHOS gathers sensitive information through the collection and analysis of multiple information sources. While ALTHOS does not spy on companies or purchase confidential information, the same sensitive information can be acquired through a creative private analysis.

The sources of information used by ALTHOS typically come from tele-interviewing industry analysts, employees, former employees, competitors, vendors, customers, industry experts, headhunters, information databases, regulatory filings, and other information sources. ALTHOS develops a unique research strategy that targets likely sources of information.

ALTHOS divides a research project into phases. Multiple sources of information are typically used for each phase as a single point of contact are rarely able to provide is the needed information. ALTHOS pieces small portions of information together to create the big picture and to separate fact from speculation. ALTHOS uses multiple confirming sources to ensure information accuracy. ALTHOS may make hundreds of contacts to complete a single research phase.

ALTHOS contact sources are not disclosed to the client. ALTHOS does not solicit or purchase information that is marked confidential or proprietary. However, using our research processes, ALTHOS receives similar information that is not marked confidential.

Do you want to get more information or have an expert help you to understand how to use your data networks or the Internet to reduce your telecommunications costs?

Consider using Althos to educate you or your staff on the implementation and technologies used to connect telephones through data networks. Althos offers onsite courses, public courses, and real-time web seminar training. If you want instruction from experts who have setup Internet telephone systems, consider Althos. Althos can customize training to cover your key subject areas. Althos also has standard courses including:

VoIP for Executives

What a management team should know about the costs and risks of sending voice through data networks.

VoIP for Operation Managers

The operation details that operation managers need to know about selecting, implementing, and managing systems that send voice through data networks.

VoIP for Telecom Professionals

The technical information for telecommunication professionals who need to understand competing technologies and how telecommunications systems are adapting to meet the changes.

- On-Site Instruction • Individual Enrollment
- Online Training • Custom Courses

About Althos

Althos provides unbiased information to consumers and business to help them discover select, and implement alternative communication technologies and systems. Althos performs research, analysis, testing, and provides education courses and books.

Althos Training, 404 Wake Chapel Road, Fuquay-Varina NC 27526 USA
1-919-557-2260 1-800-227-9681 Fax 1-919-557-2261 WWW.Althos.com

About The Instructor

Our leading instructor Lawrence Harte has 28 years of communication technology and business experience. He has worked with hundreds of people and companies to help them setup Internet telephone and voice over data network services. As of 2003, Mr. Harte had authored over 30 books and industry research reports on telecommunications technologies and communication business systems. Mr. Harte holds degrees of Executive MBA from Wake Forest University and a BSET from the University of the State of New York. He has instructed at and received numerous certificates from many university and non-university courses including VoIP/Internet Telephony, 3G wireless, wireless billing, Bluetooth technology, Internet billing, communications, cryptograph, microwave measurement and calibration, radar, nuclear power, Dale Carnegie, 360 leadership, and public speaking.

Mr. Harte has appeared on television as an industry expert and has been referenced in over 75 telecommunications related articles in industry magazines. He has been a speaker and moderator at numerous industry seminars and trade shows. His magazine publications include Popular Science, Wireless Week, RCR, Cellular Business, Cellular Marketing and others. Between 1993-1995, he wrote a monthly column in Cellular Marketing called "Techniques." The monthly Techniques column explained the business related issues behind key technology innovations that were developing in the telecommunications industry. Mr. Harte has worked for leading communication companies including Ericsson/General Electric, Audiovox/Toshiba, and TSAI/Westinghouse. He has consulted and been an expert witness for companies including AT&T, Nokia, Hughes Network Systems, Ameritech, Casio, Ericsson, Gateway, Samsung, Sony, AMD, VLSI, Siemens and many others.

Typical Training Costs

On-Site Training

Althos on-site training cost ranges from $2,200 to $3,600 per day of instruction plus expenses dependent on the length of the course and the type of content (labs, exercise materials, and instructor skill level). Althos does not charge for instructor travel time.

If Althos must incur travel expenses in conjunction with the project (this is typical for an on-site training session or presentation), travel expenses will be reimbursed on the basis of actual cost. The client prior to commitment will approve all travel expenses.

Online Training (Web Seminars)

Althos provides some courses and executive briefings in the form of online web seminars. Althos web training seminars allow two-way audio with all the participants along with presentation materials. The typical cost of web seminars range from about $85 for a 1-hour open enrollment executive briefing to approximately $350 per day for standard course instruction.

Open Enrollment

Althos periodically offers open enrollment to allow individuals to attend courses. The typical cost for individual enrollment ranges from $1,100 to $1,800 per student dependent on the location and type of course. Open enrollment courses include meals and materials (books and workbooks).

Custom Course Development

Althos can customize our courses to meet your specific training need or we can research and use our materials to create a new course. Custom course development fees range from $50 to $200 per presentation slide (graphics + descriptive text).

Internet Telephone Books

by ALTHOS Publishing

Internet Telephone Basics

ISBN: 0-9728053-0-3 Price: $29.95
Author: Lawrence Harte
#Pages: 226   Copyright Year: 2003

Internet Telephone Basics explains how and why people and companies are changing to Internet Telephone Service. Learn how much money can be saved using Internet telephone service and how you can to use standard telephones and dial the same way. Internet telephone service usually costs 1.5 to 4 cents/min for long distance calls and 3 to 10 cents/min for International calls. It describes how to activate Internet telephone service instantly and how to display your call details on the web. Covered are the advanced features and services including intelligent call forwarding, unified email and voice mail messaging, and the simultaneous sending of voice, data, and video through the Internet during your calls.

Internet Telephone Illustrated Dictionary

ISBN: 0-9728053-1-1 Price: $39.95
Author: Lawrence Harte
#Pages 750 Copyright Year: 2003

The Internet Telephone Illustrated Dictionary provides definitions and illustration the latest voice over data and Internet telephone technologies and provides the understanding needed to communicate with others in the telecommunications industry. It contains over 10,000 of the latest voice over data definitions, more than 4,000+ of the latest industry terms and acronyms, includes and introduction to Internet telephone technology, uses 400+ diagrams to help explain complex definitions, and contains directories of magazines, associations and other essential trade resources. This book is an essential reference book for those involved in all aspects of the Internet and voice over data network (VoIP) industry.

Voice over Data Networks for Managers

ISBN: 0-9728053-2-X Price: $49.95
Author: Lawrence Harte
#Pages: 352 Copyright Year: 2003

Voice over Data Networks for Managers explains how to reduce communication costs 40% to 70%, keep existing telephone systems, and ways to increase revenue from new communication applications. Discover the critical steps companies should take and risks to avoid when transitioning from private telephone systems (KTS, PBX, and CTI) to provide voice over data (VoIP) services. Understand IP Centrex and Internet PBX (iPBX) systems and the different types of telephones, call servers and features they use. Learn how to get the necessary quality of service (QoS), security, and reliability you expect from traditional telephone systems.

Althos Publishing, 404 Wake Chapel Road, Fuquay NC 27526 USA
1-919-557-2260 1-800-227-9681 Fax 1-919-557-2261 WWW.Althos.com
Email: Info@Althos.com

Printed in the United States
23922LVS00001B/169-206